ad:

oZ

CWS

and London

Crews, Donald
We read: A to Z

A new concept in alphabet books. A is for
almost and Z is for zigzag.

B 19-477

Particularly for Ann, Ninā, Amy, Donna, Janine, Michael, and Zönke

From the alphabet, with just twenty-six letters, A to Z, all words are made.

Aa, almost: nearly all red

1

Bb, bottom: where the green is

2

Cc, corner: where the yellow is

3

Dd, double: always two, always the same

4

Ee, equal: as many black as yellow

5

Ff, few:
not many
squares

6

Gg, grow: things get bigger

7

Hh, horizontal: from side to side

8

Ii, inside:
where the
black is

9

Jj, jagged: sharp points

10

Kk, kind:
same shape,
different
color

11

Ll, left:
the half
where the
blue is

12

Mm, middle: the center from any direction

13

Nn, nothing:

14

Oo, over: where the black is

15

Pp, parts: pieces separated

16

Qq, quarters: four equal parts

17

Rr, right:
the half
where the
blue is

18

Ss, size:
one large,
one small

19

Tt, top: where the blue is

20

Uu, under: where the black is

Vv, vertical: up and down

22

Ww, whole:
in one piece

23

Xx, extra: one square left over

24

Yy, only: just one

25

Zz, zigzag: looks as it sounds

26